Photography: Thomas Brodman, Helmut Dietz, Heinrich Dröge, Günter Ott, Arnulf Oyen, and Rico Pfirstinger.

Originally published in German by Kynos Verlag, Dr. Dieter Fleig, GmbH, under the title *Huskies in Action, Die Faszination Des Schlittenhundesports*. First edition ©1993 by Kynos Verlag, Dr. Dieter Fleig GmbH, Am Remelsbach 30, D-54570 Murlenbach/Eifel.

Distributed in the UNITED STATES to the Pet Trade by T.F.H. Publications, Inc., One T.F.H. Plaza, Neptune City, NJ 07753; distributed in the UNITED STATES to the Bookstore and Library Trade by National Book Network, Inc. 4720 Boston Way, Lanham MD 20706; in CANADA to the Pet Trade by H & L Pet Supplies Inc., 27 Kingston Crescent, Kitchener, Ontario N2B 2T6; Rolf C. Hagen Ltd., 3225 Sartelon Street, Montreal 382 Quebec; in CANADA to the Book Trade by Vanwell Publishing Ltd., 1 Northrup Crescent, St. Catharines, Ontario L2M 6P5 ; in ENGLAND by T.F.H. Publications, PO Box 15, Waterlooville PO7 6BQ; in AUSTRALIA AND THE SOUTH PACIFIC by T.F.H. (Australia), Pty. Ltd., Box 149, Brookvale 2100 N.S.W., Australia; in NEW ZEALAND by Brooklands Aquarium Ltd. 5 McGiven Drive, New Plymouth, RD1 New Zealand; in Japan by T.F.H. Publications, Japan—Jiro Tsuda, 10-12-3 Ohjidai, Sakura, Chiba 285, Japan; in SOUTH AFRICA by Lopis (Pty) Ltd., P.O. Box 39127, Booysens, 2016, Johannesburg, South Africa. Published by T.F.H. Publications, Inc.
MANUFACTURED IN THE UNITED STATES OF AMERICA
BY T.F.H. PUBLICATIONS, INC.

HUSKIES
IN
ACTION

THE FASCINATION OF DOGSLEDDING

by
Rico Pfirstinger

Acknowledgments

People who write books used to suffer agonies when faced with a blank piece of paper–today, it is the blank computer screen. But it also takes much more than the work of one person to fill it up.

I owe thanks first and foremost to the many people active in the sport who have answered my questions and shared their experiences with me. Here, I would like to single out Lutz Binzer and Heini Winter. I thank them for their patience and also for my first experience on a sled.

A well-deserved rest at Sils. (1993)

Ernst Müller was kind enough to give me his material on the history of sled dog racing.

I do not want to omit my friend and colleague Thomas Brodmann, whose photographic cooperation I learned to treasure, particularly at the 1991 Alpirod.

Finally, I owe thanks to the manufacturers of my photographic equipment for the quick repairs to my repeatedly misused tools.

Sincere thanks to everyone who helped: Lutz Binzer, Thomas Brodmann, Bernd Dahlke, Helmut Dietz, Heinrich Dröge, Dieter Emhofer, Dr. Dieter Fleig, Hans Huber, Florian Jochum, Marcello Kolmberger, Günther and Harald Longo, Martinus Martin, Ernst Müller, Günter Ott, Arnulf Oyen, Arthur Philipp, Karl-Heinz Raubuch, Franz Röckl, Dietrich Umlauf, and Heini Winter.

Title page: *"Leika," a Siberian Husky.*

6

Contents

Foreword

Each year during sled dog races, tens of thousands of people are fascinated by the strength, elegance, and endurance of the best husky teams. Without question, the main attraction is the animals.

In our area, sled dogs have been around for about 40 years. In Alaska, however, they won their place long ago. At first, they were used in hunting and to pull loads; later, small-scale competitions were set up at gatherings. From these competitions, ultimately, emerged the different categories of sprint, medium-distance and long-distance races.

In Europe, when I began sled dog racing in the mid-eighties, you could use only purebred huskies. Everything was in its infancy then, and there was no such thing as prize money. As the years passed, this changed, and in the meantime, a star that is not a purebred—the Alaskan Husky—has taken over here too, as the fastest and most tireless sled dog.

The best European teams are now evenly matched with their competitors from Canada and Alaska. Europe has caught up–this is clear from the fact that the sprint championship is now held alternately in Europe and North America.

Sled dogs have a pronounced pack instinct—they love nothing more than running with their fellows in a team. Out in front, of course, is the lead dog, an especially intelligent animal that has gained its position as a result of countless kilometers of training. And finally, a team's performance and success in competition depends on the men and women on the sled, who must show a very special love and concern for their animals.

Good sled dogs are without question among the best cared for and trained animal athletes in the world. Under ideal conditions, they are capable of performances that never fail to surprise even myself. It is a unique, even indescribable, feeling to glide along an icy trail with a large team of 18 to 20 optimally trained huskies.

Whether you are on the sled yourself or just want to participate in the world of the husky as an observer, this book will give you an up-close look at this fascinating, many-faceted sport.

Hans Gatt

Opposite page:
Hans Gatt is one of the most successful sprint mushers and one of the few Europeans to have made sled dog racing into a profession. Today, the Austrian is living and training in British Columbia, Canada. This photo, taken in 1992, shows him at the finish line in Bad Mitterndorf, where he won the World Championship (WC) title in the Open Class.

Introduction

Sled dogs–at the very mention of the words, who does not think of the endless vastness of Alaska, the traditional way of life of northern peoples, and polar scientists and adventurers, who were taken to the end of the world by their huskies?

Today, snowmobiles and airplanes have taken over these jobs. And yet, the sled dog is still around. Even though a dog's master no longer depends on it for survival, the animal still serves as friend and companion.

As times changed, huskies were discovered for sport. In Alaska, sled dog races soon developed into huge media events. The best known is surely the Iditarod, the longest and, thanks to many books and films, also the best-documented race in the world.

Sled dogs are found in Central Europe, too. More than 50 years ago, we imported our first animals from Scandinavia and North America and began to breed them systematically. In all breeds of sled dogs you will find true work and sport dogs, as well as "show dogs" bred for exhibition.

Within the last ten years, trained racing sled dogs-Alaskan Huskies-have been imported from Alaska and North America. They are especially fast, powerful dogs, which differ considerably from one another in appearance—in size, color, markings, and so on. There are no special standards for breeding them; the main criteria are characteristics such as speed, endurance, intelligence, and friendliness toward humans. Consequently, you will not find the Alaskan Husky at a breed show, but you will see it at the most demanding races in the world. Nowadays, both the established sled dog breeds and the Alaskan Huskies have been bred beyond their traditional characteristics.

Sled dog races have mushroomed during the last ten years, quickly metamorphosing to become a magnet for the public–in Italy, France, the Netherlands, and, in particular, in the German-speaking Alpine region. The European sled dog sport is winning new friends daily. As it does so, local events–at least when they exploit the positive aspects of the home territory–are every bit a match for the formerly superior rivals in Alaska and North America. The 1992 Sprint World Championship in Bad Mitterndorf saw, in addition to the fifth-highest attendance figures, gold medals for Europe in all classes–the favorites from North America had to admit defeat.

Opposite page:
Dog weather. Snow flurries at the 1992 World Championship in Bad Mitterndorf. The dogs are tied up at the "stake-out," the area where they wait until it is their team's turn to start.

No doubt about it: sled dog racing is well established here, too, and reports in the news media create growing interest among the public and sponsors as well. In Germany alone, more than 1,500 so-called mushers harness their huskies to sleds or pulkas. As early as September, you see sportsmen on their training wagons tearing along paths in field and forest.

An active sled dog is undoubtedly happier than one of its fellows that has to spend its life in a kennel or another kind of cramped quarters. And happily, in Europe, the sled dog sport has thus far, in spite of increased popularity, been spared the negative developments that can be observed in other kinds of sports involving animals. The main reason for this is that huskies really do pull sleds willingly, without the "help" of reins or whips. Moreover, the veterinarians for racing dogs make sure that not one sick or injured animal will be sent out on the trail.

Puppy at Pfitsch. (training camp, 1992)

Once you have seen a race, you know the boundless enthusiasm a husky has for pulling a sled. It is a task best performed in company with its pack mates. Dogs and musher form an inseparable bond, and all sides get their own kind of enjoyment from it.

However, this pretty picture might change one day. In some areas, bigger prizes and wealthier sponsors have already led to commercial husky "factories," which produce as many as 100 pups each season and bury the less well-endowed "outcasts" in the woods. Not much is left of the idealism of earlier times.

In Europe, fortunately, the situation is different. We hope that things stay this way, and that, in the future, this unusual sport remains immune to greed and the search for recognition at the animals' expense.

Opposite page:
Trying for the record. Heini Winter's team at the start in Buchenberg. Eighteen Alaskan Huskies pull the sled over the 20-km-long sprint trail, where, at the same time, the world record for the fastest-run kilometer will be measured. (1992)

Twins. A handsome husky duo at Nassereith. (1991)

Huskies and Mushers

It all began in Alaska. Around the turn of the century, the city of Nome, on the Bering Sea, was a booming gold town. In 1899, the news that the yellow metal had been found spread like wildfire, and within a few years, 20,000 people had made their way to Nome, hoping to make their fortunes at the mouth of the Yukon River. During the winter, the only available transportation was dog sled. Every single thing people needed–food, mail, construction materials, and equipment–was brought in by dog teams. It is not surprising, then, that during the winter, gold miners and prospectors began to stage short races among themselves, especially since there was no way one could dig for gold in the frozen ground.

As early as 1908, the first official competition took place: the All-Alaska Sweepstakes. The trail followed the telegraph lines from Nome to Candle and back again, the total distance a considerable 408 miles.

So it was that the modern sport of dog-sledding was born, and it developed so successfully that husky teams were allowed as a demonstration sport at the 1932 Winter Olympics held at Lake Placid, February 6 and 7. The winner of the gold medal was the Canadian musher Emile St. Godard and his mixed team of Russian Wolfhounds and Alaskan Malamutes.

Why are the sled drivers called mushers? Early Franco-Canadian dog sledders used to spur their dogs on with the command "Marche." To their English-speaking followers, that sounded like "Mush." Dog-sledders eventually came to be known as mushers.

Sled dogs also entered Europe, by way of Scandinavia. In 1931, the Norsk Trekkhundklubb came into being, followed three years later by the Swensk Draghundklubb, in Sweden. Here began the so-called pulkasport: a team pulled a weighted frame (20 kilos for each animal) while the dog driver followed on skis. Dogs, frame, and musher were tied together with lines. The distance covered by a pulka varies between 5 km for relay races to 30 km for national championships. The sled dogs are usually short-haired animals bred from ordinary hunting and work dogs. In Scandinavia, pulka racing became enormously popular, and today, more than 150,000 people are active in the sport.

The "classic" form of husky sport–using racing sleds instead of

Opposite page:
Harmony. Anja Hörmann poses at Sils with husky, sled, and mascot. (1993)

pulkas–began in Central Europe with the founding of the Schweizerischen Klubs fur Nordische Hunde (Nordic Dog Club of Switzerland) in 1959. The goal of the SKNH was "the advancement of care and breeding of Nordic dogs." Included in this category, in addition to the many breeds of Nordic hunting dogs and watchdogs, of course, were the classic sled dog breeds: Alaskan Malamute, Greenland Dog, Samoyed, and Siberian Husky.

In January 1970, also in Switzerland, Central Europe's first organized sled dog race took place. Three years later, the Trail Club of Europe (TCE)– the first Central European sled dog club–was formed. Like their models in America, the races held by the TCE and its sister organizations were met with great success. Toward the end of the seventies, the new sport had taken hold in most European countries. The rapid growth cried out for an "umbrella" organization. Since its founding in 1983, the European Sled Dog Racing Association (ESDRA) has functioned as the umbrella organization for sled dog sports and instituted the annual European championships.

Much more interesting than the development of organizations and clubs, of course, are the changes that occurred in the main actors– the sled dogs themselves. Until the beginning of the 1980s, there were only four registered sled dog breeds in Central Europe. This was completely understandable since the sport had, after all, evolved from the dog breeding clubs. Things were altogether different in America: there, the Alaskan Husky dominated the picture–fast-performance crossbreds quickly drove the purebred animals from the front ranks. A few mushers began to introduce these mixed breeds into Europe and to raise them there–and purebred teams were faced with powerful competition.

At first, Alaskan Huskies imported into Europe still had to be provided with "artificial" pedigrees in order to qualify for participation in official races. In 1986, therefore, the clubs that composed the ESDRA agreed to adapt to the international norm and to open their events to unregistered dogs, too.

This was a decision with significant consequences. Many mushers who owned purebreds now felt themselves at a disadvantage and, in 1986/87 founded new organizations whose races could be entered only by dogs of the four registered breeds. This division is still in effect today: In almost every Central European country there are some sled dog races open to all types of huskies and others limited to purebred teams. There are even two competing European

Championships. Of these, the open version held by the ESDRA is certainly the more interesting from the sports point of view.

The first World Championship in the sprint was held in 1990 in St. Moritz, with around 700 dogs participating. A year later the event was held in Winnipeg, Canada, and since then the World Championship has been held alternately in Europe and North America. Teams participate in several categories: in addition to pulka racers, there is one class for up to four dogs, one for up to six, and one for up to eight. The undisputed "king" of the events is the open class with any number of huskies–many entrants harness up as many as 22 animals. Often, real acrobatics are required to guide the almost 20-meter-long team safely through the tight curves. There is no room for mistakes, because if the musher falls off his sled, the dogs will just keep on running.

The courses covered during Sprint World Championship are relatively short: depending on the class, they vary between 5 and 25 kilometers. Long-distance courses are another matter entirely. For the Iditarod, the longest of them all, participants must cover more than 1,800 kilometers. The Alpirod is on a par with the Iditarod: this

In pulka racing, the sled dog pulls a frame weighing 44 pounds, which is connected by a rope to the musher, who follows on cross-country skis. In this sport, dominated by Scandinavians, the dogs are usually special breeds of hunting dogs. (1992 WC)

European long-distance race follows a steep mountain and valley trail through four Alpine countries in a good dozen stages to cover a total distance of up to 1,000 kilometers.

A TRAINING SESSION

Everything seemed perfect. I lay on a fantastically beautiful beach, lounging in the white sand. The gentle whisper of the surf was disturbed only occasionally by a soft sobbing, which I decided to ignore.

It wasn't working. The sobbing grew to a piercing whine, changed suddenly to an eerie whimpering, and finally broke out in a gasping howl. Sun, sea, and sand faded, and the whole scene dropped behind a jet-black curtain. I awoke.

I was lying in the musty loft of an

A team of Greenlands in its native land in the far North. Quite typical is the fan-shaped team harness (fan hitch). It offers the best protection against fissures in glaciers and is especially helpful in hunting.

old hydroelectric plant. Through the peephole above my bed the pale light of an early November morning fell on the dusty room, which was scantily heated by the exhaust from the two generators. A glance at the clock told me I had overslept. Stiff as a snake in a refrigerator, I got up and peered out the tiny window, looking for the cause of the strange sounds that had awakened me.

Down below, a ferocious battle was going on. Heini Winter–or rather his fog-enshrouded silhouette– had just begun to prepare a huge pot of meat broth for his 12 Alaskan Huskies. The frantic dogs kept jumping on him as he worked; then, to the accompaniment of a many-voiced concert of howling, growling, and whining, the dogs became a blurry tangle of scuffling bodies. I wanted to get a better look at this! I got dressed in a hurry and rushed downstairs.

In 1989, Heini Winter had taken over the DSSV (Deutschen Schlittenhundesport-Verband), the German Sled Dog Sporting Club, which was in very bad shape. Now, the club was once more in the black, attendance at races was good, and– particularly important for Heini–there were more sponsors. The truth is, the care and training of a sled dog team is a fairly expensive proposition. When you add to that the travel costs for big races or the expense of shipping dogs overseas to the World Championship in Alaska, you can imagine that the total exceeds the financial capacity of many mushers. Without sponsorship money, the DSSV would not be able to provide the necessary support for such undertakings.

At the end of 1990, I was to interview Heini Winter for a magazine, so I was glad to accept his invitation to accompany him on a training session. But by the time I had entered his hydroelectric plant in Augsburg, the day's practice rounds were over. Instead, I was able to gain deep insight into the actual work of a sled-dog master: Heini spent more than three hours with his dogs: feeding them, talking to them, playing with them, putting cream on their paws, cleaning the kennels. He devoted so much attention to each individual animal that it seemed almost excessive, as he looked for the slightest crimp in their well-being.

His wife Margit and the three children worked with the dogs, too–there wasn't really much else for them to do. Heini and his family had an agreement: Heini got all the support he needed for his time-consuming hobby but in return had to promise his wife not to participate in any races that lasted longer than a weekend. For the '91 Alpirod, however, it was understood that the agreement had to be set aside. Once in his life, Heini Winter wanted to take part in Europe's longest sled dog race.

After Heini had taken care of the dogs, we went inside. I did my interview, took a few more pictures, and got ready to leave. But Heini was not ready to let me go just like that. He had promised me a training, and a training I would get! So I ended up in the loft in order to go out with Heini and the dogs the

following morning to do a round.

I stepped outdoors. I was struck simultaneously by the morning cold and Heini's broad grin. The pack of hounds were gulping down the contents of the tin bowl. "You've hardly missed a thing," Heini said comfortingly. "I just got started five minutes ago."

I took a deep breath of the cold, damp air and gazed out over the extensive kennel system, bordered on the left by the Wertach, the small river that fed the generators of the power plant. On the other side, to my great pleasure, the rising sun was slowly eating its way through the veil of fog.

Hardly had the dogs swallowed their breakfast–the purpose of the meat broth was to compensate for the loss of fluids that would occur during the day's training–when Heini began putting on the harnesses (made of padded leather), one after the other. Each animal had its own outfit–made to fit and with its name enscribed on it. "Lobo," I read, "Schnapsi," "Bandit."

As Heini worked with the dogs, he talked to them continuously in a soft voice, assuring himself of their undivided attention. Finally, when they were all in harness, he called the animals together. Immediately, they formed a ring around him; and the whole team, including the "human lead dog" in the center, made for the trailer parked in front of the kennel door.

The trailer was built of wood and had six small transport containers on it, each with a trap door fitted with a small, barred window. I couldn't for the life of me imagine the dogs going willingly into these dark, cramped boxes, especially since two dogs had to fit into each one. I was all the more surprised to see that all Heini had to do was call a dog by name and point to one of the six openings. The dog in question, tail wagging, jumped directly into its box–a good five feet above the ground.

Heini attached the trailer to his car, and together we loaded the training wagon. The rest of the gear, a confusing tangle of lines, hooks, and straps, was already in the car. We were ready to go.

Heini Winter's training site was about three kilometers west of Augsburg, in a large forested area. If you want to train sled dogs, you need unpaved trails with no automobile traffic. If there is no snow, you work with a three–or four-wheeled, metal training wagon.

In our densely populated land, it is no simple matter to find suitable terrain, especially since everyone from the forester to the local authorities has to give permission. Might the team frighten game or horseback riders? Would the howling, unavoidable before the team takes off, bother tourists looking for a restful holiday? Reasons for denial of permission

Wagon training. If it is cold enough, mushers hitch their dogs to a training wagon as early as September, to get ready for the coming season. Wagon races are also held in regions with little snow. This photo shows a team of Alaskan Malamutes.

crop up quickly. And even very successful mushers have experienced how a permit once granted may be revoked at any time.

Heini has long since stopped counting his trophies. As one of the five best German mushers, he can look back on a long string of victories. But what is victory! Heini Winter is a man who lives for his dogs. His huskies worship him. For them, he is like a father-figure, whom they trust unconditionally and for whom they are ready to give their all–and sometimes even a little more. As a team, they are one.

Back to our training session. The

23

one I experienced consisted of a level stretch about six kilometers long. It seemed short to me–a real sprint race covers a good 20 kilometers–so I asked Heini for the reason. "Strength is more important here than endurance," he answered. "The training wagon weighs 70 kilos, and I add several concrete slabs and pull an autombile tire behind. Then there is my own weight–and today, you'll be sitting on top for ballast." As he said that, he looked me over carefully, noting every extra ounce, and observed quite matter-of-factly, "Six kilometers is more than enough."

After a short ten-minute trip, we reached our destination. We unloaded, and Heini fastened the training wagon to the trailer with a special hitch so that the dogs couldn't tear it loose. Then he let the animals out of their boxes, to allow them to move around enough to warm up. The dogs, not on a leash, romped around freely, broke out now and then in the familiar howl, but stayed close by. Meanwhile, Heini fastened the central gang line to the front of the training sled and laid it out lengthwise on the frozen ground.

The racket grew louder when Heini led his lead dog Lobo to the end of the line and hooked him up to the harness and neck band. "Line out," ordered Heini, but Lobo already knew what was going on

and had pulled the line taut. One after another the rest of the dogs were attached, the noisiest ones last to keep them from inciting the quieter ones as long as possible.

Now there was no time to lose, for the twelve bundles of energy were howling, yelping, and whimpering their heads off. With mounting excitement, the animals threw themselves into the harness and, with all their strength, tried to pull the training wagon from its anchor. In their efforts they rose up at an angle and then often landed on the wrong side of the gang line, which threatened to turn the whole bunch into a hopeless tangle. Heini called out something to me, but the nerve-wracking background of sound made it impossible to understand. He signaled to me to hop up onto a basketlike contraption made of rusty iron pipe–on closer inspection, it turned out to be a tiny seat.

I was not quite settled when Heini released the anchor line. With a great lurch we catapulted forward– in spite of the additional weight, the dogs accelerated the sled from nothing to 40 kilometers per hour. The huskies galloped, and with every bound, "Moose" and "Astore," the wheel dogs attached directly to the front of the wagon, threw up a handful of sharp pebbles, which pelted my face like buckshot. I squinted and saw something that made me extremely uncomfortable:

100 meters ahead, an iron gate was blocking the way. The dogs could easily make it through underneath, but what about us? The only alternative was a right-angled detour just before it. All I heard from Heini, who was standing behind me on the sled, was an encouraging "Okay" and "Bravo" as he called to his dogs. Didn't he see the danger looming before us?

But Lobo knew what he was doing and, without losing speed, swerved to the right along the familiar trail. We'll end up in the dirt, I thought, as the wagon skidded around the corner at high speed and I was nearly torn from my seat. But I had underestimated the extraordinary stability of our vehicle: while I was ready to fly off onto the embankment, the four rubber-tired wheels of the wagon seemed to hold firmly to the ground.

After a few kilometers, the dogs seemed to slow down a bit, and I began to enjoy the ride enormously. But I didn't have much time left for this; for a few minutes later, the huskies had fulfilled their assigned task and taken us back in a loop to our starting place. Heini jammed on the brakes; the dogs reluctantly slowed down and finally came to a standstill.

The dogs stood there in their harnesses, tongues hanging out, panting, their coats soaking wet, their eyes shining. Heini filled a bowl with cold beef broth and held it up to the dogs' noses, one pair after another. There was only a little for each dog, but it was enough to cool them off and compensated somewhat for their loss of fluids. Only then were the huskies unharnessed. We allowed ourselves plenty of time; the dogs had to cool off gradually. Besides, there was lots to do: the tangle of lines and harnesses had to be sorted out and the training wagon had to be reloaded.

Back home, Margit met us with a large pot of hot coffee. Later, Heini got out a worn photo album and shared some of his memories with me. He told about his time in Canada, his dream country, where he had spent four years traveling and canoeing before returning to Augsburg in 1978. His luggage included two Siberian Huskies–the beginning of a passion. Shortly thereafter he got married and bought the hydroelectric plant, which left him enough time for his hobby and assured his family of a good income. Around the mid-eighties, Heini, like many other mushers, switched to the faster Alaskan Huskies.

Finally it was time to say goodbye. Heini and I left the house together. He was drawn again to his dogs, wanting to make sure that everything was all right. I left behind a satisfied man, one lucky enough to have two families.

Above and right:
Home advantage. If you are serious about the sport of sled-dog racing, you usually find little time for your actual profession. Heini Winter has it good: his hydroelectric plant leaves him enough free time for family and dogs.

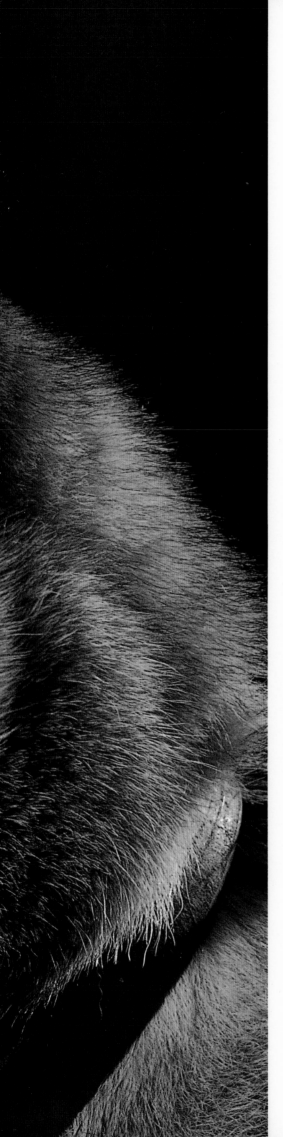

White giant. One of Peter Fromm's white Alaskan Huskies during summer vacation. In the daytime, the animals run free in vast kennels and are with their owner for hours every day. At night, they are tied up so that fights don't start.

Legendary. How did humans get sled dogs? An Eskimo myth says that the earth broke into two pieces. All the animals fled to safety except one: the dog. In despair, it struggled to avoid falling into the abyss. A man saw its precarious position and called out to it "Come." The dog sprang back and ran to the man, and has remained with him ever since. (Photo: Heini Winter with his dogs)

"Arrow," a ten-month-old Siberian Husky.

All action. Alaskan Huskies enjoy the race as much as do the mushers. (Haidmühle, 1993)

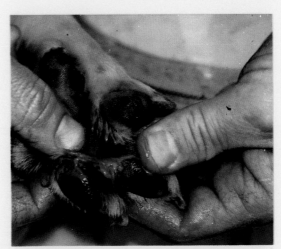

Care of the paws is an essential element of the work of any sled dog owner. Huskies' paws, under considerable stress, are treated with special creams and pastes to guard against cracks and infections.

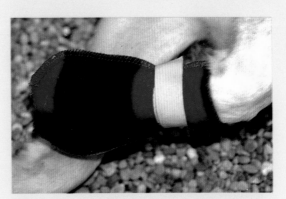

"Bootie time." Little cloth booties protect the huskies' paws from injuries–caused in winter by icy trails and in summer by sharp stones.

The last howl. Huskies are tense during the seconds before the start of a run, and they let the world know it by keeping up a continuous howling, whining, and yelping. Whether it's an important race or, as in this photo, only Lutz Binzer's evening training session in the mountains makes no difference.

Devoted companions. Lutz Binzer's dogs accept him completely as their master.

Mountain training. In a hut in the Oberallgäu, Lutz Binzer prepares his animals for Europe's longest sled dog race. At night, the huskies sleep in the stable.

They Run until They Drop!

Bad Mitterndorf is buried in snow. All night long it snowed heavily between the Dachsteingruppe and the Toten Gerbirge, and now an endless stream of cars is laboring along the poorly cleared main highway. Their goal is the Kulmer ski-flying hill, at the base of which is the starting post of the most important sled dog race of the season.

A little later on, folksinging is heard. Thousands of spectators have come. They spread out along the ropes lining the trail, cluster around huts selling mulled wine, or get refreshments in the main tent. You see fathers carrying their children on their shoulders, flags fluttering in the wind, and the voice from the loudspeaker can scarcely be heard over the howling of the dogs: "Ladies and gentlemen, welcome to the 1992 Sled Dog World Championship."

At the stake-out area, the mushers are making their final preparations: getting the sleds ready, testing lines, harnessing dogs...Finally, the dog handlers lead the assembled team to the starting line. There, the noisy animals strain wildly in their harnesses and leap toward the children as shouts of approval fill the air. Every two minutes a team starts; in one stroke, the energy expended in howling and jumping is directed forward.

From everywhere–from Central Europe, Scandinavia, the USA, Canada, and Alaska–the best teams have converged on the famous resort on the Salzkammergut highway to compare themselves and their huskies with one another, to spend three days battling for the gold. Almost without pause, deep into the afternoon, teams are starting, crossing the finish line, and still starting– until all classes have had their turn. Something is always going on at the stake-out area. The more than 2,000 huskies registered wait there for the action; there they are fed and cared for, and there, also, is every spectator who wants a closer look at these "mysterious animals." The dogs greet the spectators differently, according to how the spectator approaches them. Some are timid and fearful, others are just wild, without the least reservation. Many are noisy, others more restrained. Each sled dog has its own personality– is an individual on a team. And how they look! Large and small, slender or built like a bull, black, white, and pied–everything is there. Pulka drivers prefer short-haired hunting dogs, and the large

Opposite page:
An Alaskan Malamute, lightly dusted with snow, at the 1993 Pedigree Pal Trophy, in Bad Mitterndorf.

field of team drivers work with Alaskan Huskies of every size and color. And then there are also the purebred Siberian Huskies, admired by many spectators for their typical face mask and ice-blue eyes.

Again and again, the mushers are asked the same questions, and as time goes by, the answers become shorter and shorter: How much does a team cost? ("Lots."), What do the dogs eat? ("Practically anything.") Isn't it too warm for the poor dogs here? ("No.") How is training going? ("Great.") And so on. Of course, no one can blame the spectators for their curiosity. Communication between sled dog sports clubs and the general public is still in its infancy, so races are often the only place where accurate information can be found. But people who know what goes into keeping dogs and equipment in good shape before and after the start will understand that at those times, mushers do not have time for hour-long conversations.

Mushers are rugged individualists, anyway. Each is solely responsible for everything; some even build their own sleds. There are no service personnel to take care of broken sled runners, no outfitters to carry scientifically developed waxes, and no equipment pool to offer services to members. There isn't even a trainer! And it is usually only the owners of large teams who have a dog handler, someone who can help the musher out a little during competitions; mushers mostly rely on unpaid help from friends or family members.

Just as huskies are different, so are their different positions on the team. The strongest ones play the role of wheel dogs–they are attached directly to the front of the sled, and consequently much is demanded of

A challenge. Herbert Kohnle (six-dog class) on the jump at Buchenberg, one of the most difficult portions of the twelve-kilometer-long sprint trail.

them. If a dog is particularly teachable, persistent, and strong of nerve, it is assigned the position of lead dog. Before that, however, it often serves an apprenticeship as swing dog–right behind the lead dog, whose behavior it imitates. The rest of the dogs serve as team dogs, often for their whole racing carreer.

A lead dog is fully conscious of its exposed position, and the rest of the pack generally accepts it without question as the alpha animal. Just as with wolves, however, ranking within a pack of sled dogs is not set in stone.

The ranking animal usually rebukes a trouble-maker by confronting it with threats, such as an erect tail and ears pointing forward–signals to the upstart to watch its step. Sometimes it wants to know the challenger better and demonstrates its aggressive intentions by growling, baring its teeth, and bristling its coat. Simultaneously, the tail drops and the ears are laid back. The body language shows a cocktail of fear and aggression—the trouble-maker itself probably has doubts about a victorious outcome of the noisy display battle. Biting stops when the loser admits defeat though deferential gestures, lies down humbly on its back between the victor's legs, and tries to lick its face. This puppy-like behavior triggers an innate repression of biting in the higher-ranked animal.

As a rule, therefore, disputes over rank are usually resolved without serious injuries.

The lead dog is fully aware that its position at the head of the team is inseparably bound to the role of pack leader. Consequently, it does everything possible to please its master, who is responsible for setting it up in the first place and who can also unseat it. Sometimes this leads to a situation on the trail in which a dog exhausts itself. The rest of the pack will naturally not stay behind, and so many huskies, of their own free will, literally run until they drop. The musher, therefore, has to be able to recognize any signs of exhaustion and stop immediately to unharness the animal in question and take it in the sled bag to the finish or to the next control point, where the dog, under the watchful eye of a veterinarian, usually recovers quickly. Especially in medium-distance and long-distance races, it takes a good measure of experience to allow the team to run at a speed that optimizes its forces for the stage that lies ahead.

Training for a sled dog begins even before it is a year old. The animal learns in a playful way, following the example of older team members—whose behavior it copies. The main task of the musher is to establish a good mood, thereby insuring that the dogs enjoy their running to the utmost. If that doesn't work, watch out! A young husky that connects pulling a sled with unpleasant experiences will never give its best freely–even when it is ever so talented and well trained. For this very reason, you cannot and should not force anything. After the first months of practice, the yearlings will be carefully familiarized with the aspects of racing and will get used to the greater strain on the nerves and the hurly-burly of the whole affair.

A lead dog has special demands made on it. It must have leadership qualities in the truest sense and be able to follow the musher's commands: "Gee" for right, "Haw" for left, and in certain circumstances "Come gee" and "Come haw" for the corresponding turn-abouts. To urge the dogs on, mushers usually use "Go," "Hike," "Mush," "Allez," or, simply, "Okay." The command for stop is "Whoa," but it is seldom effective. You have to have good brakes to bring a running team to a halt.

There are lead dogs that have made history. One such dog was named Balto. Today a bronze statue of him stands in New York's Central Park. In the summer, children crawl around on his back and pull on his ears, pointed attentively toward the North. Balto was one of Leonhard Seppala's Siberian Huskies. More than 65 years ago, he took part in the so-called Serum Run and performed so heroically that hundreds of Alaskans were saved from death.

The story began in January 1925, when Dr. Curtis Welch, the only doctor in Nome, discovered a case of diphtheria. There were about 2,000 people living in Nome at the time, most of them Eskimos, who were extremely susceptible to this disease, which they called the "black death." An epidemic was in the making, and the only supply of antitoxin was 900 miles away, in Anchorage. In view of the unpredictable weather conditions, transport by airplane–unreliable biplanes with open cockpits– seemed too uncertain. So the vaccine was loaded in a special train that took it 225 miles north to Nenana, where the tracks of the Alaskan Railroad came to an end.

From there, there was only one solution: sled dogs. Twenty teams stood ready along the way from Nenana to Nome to carry the life-saving drug in stages, at breakneck speed, to its destination. The race against time began late in the evening of January 27. The temperature was 45 degrees below zero when the postmaster, William "Wild Bill" Shannon, stowed the package of serum, which weighed about 22 pounds and was wrapped in cloths and hides, on his sled and took off on the first leg of the journey.

At the same time, Leonhard Seppala, 674 miles away in Nome,

departed to meet the mushers as they made their way west along the Tenana and Yukon rivers. Since the turn of the century, Seppala, a Norwegian by birth, had worked his way up to become Alaska's best-known musher. Most of his dogs were Siberian Huskies, and his lead dogs, Balto and Togo, had already won many races. In Bluff, Seppala left Balto and some of the other dogs behind so that they could rest there until it was time for the return journey. Farther along, on Norton Sound, Seppala ran into one of the blizzards typical of this part of the world; luckily for him, it was blowing at his back.

Finally he met up with Henry Ivanoff, the sixteenth-stage driver, who transferred the serum to him. Seppala immediately began the return journey and, to save time, decided to take the dangerous route across the frozen sea. The temperature had risen, and he could hear the ice breaking around him. Now the winds were blowing so hard in his face that he could no longer see Togo at the head of the team. But Togo, like Balto, had proved himself on countless trails; he understood the danger and grasped Seppala's commands before he could even utter them. Nonetheless, it was a small miracle that the team reached Golovin safely, after 84 miles at breakneck speed. There, Charlie Olson took over the life-saving package to carry

it to Bluff, 25 miles farther on. The storm blew his team off course several times, and Olson suffered a frostbitten hand. But he persisted.

In Bluff, Gunnar Kasson took up the journey–with the dogs that Seppala had left behind on his way out. Balto ran at the lead, fighting his way through the blizzard that hit the team with winds of 78 miles per hour. Kasson lost his way and missed Ed Rohn, who was waiting in Safety to take the last lap. The fate of the people of Nome now depended solely on Balto, who pointed his head downward and seemed to sniff out the trail, deeply buried in snow.

What happened next is uncertain. People say that the sled tipped over, dumping the serum into the snow, and that Kasson had to go after it with his bare hands. In any event, early in the morning of February 2, a half-frozen Gunnar Kasson staggered into Dr. Welch's office, gave him the package containing the frozen but still effective serum, and at once went outside again. He collapsed beside his exhausted team and began to remove the ice from Balto's paws. "Balto..." he is said to have murmured, "...damn good dog."

A dog as exceptional as Balto does not turn up every day. You might find one like him at the Iditarod, the longest–and many claim also the most difficult–sled dog race in the world. From

Anchorage to Nome, it covers a good 1,100 miles, long stretches of it covering the same trail used on the Serum Run. In fact, there are two alternate routes: one to the North for the even years and one to the South for odd years. Along both trails, a number of control points have been set up, where mushers find water, straw, and supplies that they left there before the race. "There is nothing in the world like the Iditarod," wrote the American musher and sports journalist Tim Mowry. "For two long weeks, it is as if you were on another planet. After you have run the Iditarod, life seems boring." The US television network ABC saw to it that these pictures from another planet were carried to every living room in America. The whole of Alaska catches Iditarod fever and turns its gaze on its new heroes. And so it should: the Iditarod is difficult, tricky, and truly dangerous... "The Last Great Race on Earth," as the sponsor promises. Many an inexperienced participant has put his life, and naturally the lives of his dogs, on the line.

To do well in the Iditarod, you need more than just good huskies. Often the proper tactics are also critical, so the mushers spend lots of time studying the state of health of competing teams. Is there a slight outbreak of infection that would weaken the opponent's team? And then the weather reports: Should

one venture out in a predicted storm or better wait and give the dogs their well-earned rest? Many pretend to go to sleep at the control point and then set out on the trail secretly. Others sleep in hidden places or hide the alarm clock beneath their heavy cap so that the competition doesn't get wind of what they are up to. And through the press and other channels, many participants intentionally spread false information so as to confuse their opponents.

If you believe several-time Iditarod winner Rick Swenson, only once in his life might a musher come across a truly outstanding lead dog. Susan Butcher, who has also won the Iditarod several times, is of quite the opposite point of view. In her opinion, good sled dogs do not fall from heaven–they are made. "Breeding is not the main thing," she explains. "Other mushers have dogs with outstanding genes, too. The problem is not in choosing the right genes but rather what happens to a husky after it is born. A sled dog with second-class genes and first-class training will always beat one with first-class genes and second-class training. The whole thing is not magic but work, work, and more work." So much for the pragmatic approach of an ambitious and thoroughly successful woman who has owned more than 140 sled dogs.

Such superlatives are difficult to translate to our conditions here in Europe–the difference between the vastness of America and our densely settled lands, where sometimes there are enormous difficulties in keeping just one dog, is too great. Maybe that is all to the good. Who knows what the life of any given husky is worth in Alaska, and how many so-called "second rate" pups do not survive their first year there?

In Europe, amateur mushers drive with the dogs they have, and this leads necessarily to a somewhat more relaxed attitude with regard to winning. People do not depend on winning in unnatural ways, with drugged or otherwise stressed dogs. A "professional" musher might need such victories to put himself and his sponsors in the media limelight or to defray his expenses with prize money or the sale of dogs.

For European sled dog sports, then, the title "amateur" takes on a completely new meaning. It stands for small, personal, cleanly won victories, the opposite of the dividends of live television broadcasting.

Meanwhile, it is afternoon in Bad Mitterndorf. The crowds around the ropes at the finish line have disappeared, the loudspeakers are quiet, and the last spectator is making his way to the victory ceremony. But one team is still out. Finally it appears on the home stretch–three powerful Alaskan Malamutes in harness, followed by a musher who seems to be counting every single meter between him and his goal. The sled glides leisurely across the finish line and comes to a stop. Finished! The musher walks to the front of his team, kneels, and strokes his lead dog tenderly on the head. Then, he picks up its paws and begins to remove the ice.

You don't have to be a Balto to be a hero.

On the short leash. At the stake-out, a network of chains and steel lines, every musher can leave his huskies outdoors before the start. In big races, often more than a thousand dogs come together, and they quickly break out into a howling, yelping, ear-splitting chorus.

Endurance. The team of Switzerland's Ivan Schmidt in action. Although the six huskies in this photo have already run a good ten kilometers, not a single sign of fatigue is evident. (1992 WC)

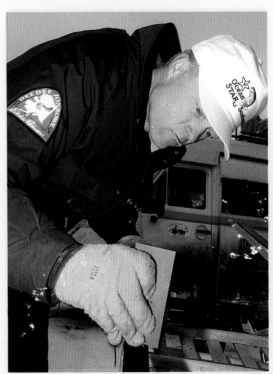

Getting ready for the race. Proper preparation of equipment is just as important as well-trained dogs. This photo shows Deedee Jonrowe's dog handler waxing the runners. (Alpirod, 1992)

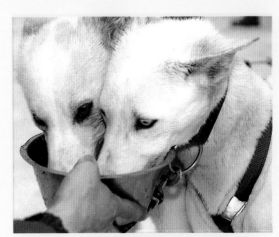

Right after crossing the finish line, the huskies are given a bowl of cold meat broth to compensate for fluid loss. (Heini Winter's team at the 1992 WC)

Before the very start of the race, helpers join forces to hold the sled back. In this photo: Anja Hörmann at the Pedigree Pal Trophy in Bad Mitterndorf. (1993)

Power slide. Helmut Peer of Austria leans hard into a turn. (Bad Mitterndorf, 1993)

Worn out. At the end of a race, many mushers are more exhausted than are their dogs. (Bad Mitterndorf, 1993)

A scuffle. Sometimes fights erupt at the stake-out. The musher tries his best to arrange the chains in such a way that only animals that get along well can come in contact with one another. (WC, 1992)

Although hybrids have come to dominate the sled dog scene, the Siberian Husky is still the most graceful and elegant of all sled dogs.

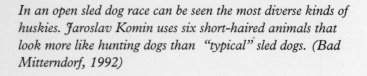

In an open sled dog race can be seen the most diverse kinds of huskies. Jaroslav Komin uses six short-haired animals that look more like hunting dogs than "typical" sled dogs. (Bad Mitterndorf, 1992)

Above and bottom right:
A sponsor's hot-air balloon gives journalists and spectators the chance to experience sled dog racing from a different perspective. (Sils, 1993)

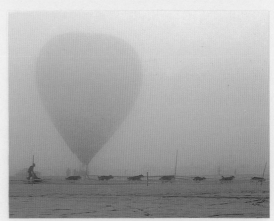

Limited visibility for this musher and his team in Kötschach-Mauthen, Austria. (1993)

"They're off!" Alaskan huskies at work. (Haidmühle, 1993)

Sled dog racing has a strong following. Even at smaller races, such as here in Haidmühle, several thousand spectators often line the trail.

Race sponsor representatives Gabi and Dagmar are on hand to see that all goes as smoothly as possible. (European Championship, Pfitsch, 1993)

Who will win? Countless spectators are present at the drawing for a four-wheel-drive vehicle. (Pedigree Pal Trophy, Bad Mitterndorf, 1993)

Countdown … Seconds before the start, huskies hungry to run are held back by a helper. (Haidmühle)

With lightweight wooden sleds coming into use in sprint races, a musher can master tight, difficult spots—if he is agile enough. (Buchenberg, 1992)

Nap time. Huskies are taken to races in special trailers fitted with small compartments. The close quarters make perfect sense—the animals are protected from injury on curving highways. (Nassereith, 1991)

Off and running. Josef Rinkel has huskies of every color on his team. (Bad Mitterndorf, 1992)

Huskies, like human marathon runners, sometimes overestimate their strength. A responsible musher notices this immediately, takes the exhausted dog aboard the sled, and carries it to the finish line. A veterinarian waits there, just in case. (Bad Mitterndorf, 1992)

In the four-dog category, Germany's Volkmar Stuber is in a class by himself—for years, he held the European and World Championship titles. This photo shows the medalist musher on the way to the gold medal at the 1992 WC.

Trail's end. Its dense undercoat makes this husky, sleeping at the stake-out, immune to the cold. (Bad Gastein, 1991)

A musher and his dog make themselves comfortable after the race. (Pedigree Pal Trophy, Sils, 1993)

Above and below:
Husky pups play as hard as they can—thereby becoming socialized for later life in the pack. (Above: Sils; below: Haidmühle)

Devotion. Terry Streeper of Canada, winner of the first Pedigree Pal Trophy, as well as the European and World Championships in the Open Class, can rely on his dogs. Even after two strenuous days of racing, his animals show him their unwavering affection. (Bad Mitterndorf, 1993)

Crowd-pleaser. Terry Streeper gives out autographs. (Bad Mitterndorf, 1993)

Top speed. Terry Streeper at the start of the race at Sils. (Pedigree Pal Trophy, 1993)

Terry Streeper going full speed with his huge 20-dog team in the Pedigree Pal Trophy at Sils. (1993)

A matter of form. Mushers have a lot to do on the trail too; they help the team along by "pedaling"–pushing off with their feet. (Pedigree Pal Trophy, Sils, 1993)

Before a start, sled dogs are often so intent on running that they jump all over each other and get tangled up. Dog handlers then have the thankless task of untangling them in time.

A musher petting his dogs for a job well done. (Sils, 1993)

A Thousand Kilometers through the Alps

"Thirty seconds!" The voice from the loudspeaker sounds blasé. But Lutz Binzer is fired up. Every nerve tensed, the 50-year-old Allgäuer native stands on the runners of his sled and feverishly awaits the moment of release, when his 12 huskies will catapult him over the starting line at Sexten. It is a familiar feeling–a good feeling. For the sixth time, Binzer has taken off in January to take part in the longest sled dog race in Europe. And once again, he wants to place among the top ten.

"Ten seconds!" From all sides, helpers crowd around to hold back the dogs, now straining at their harnesses, to keep them from pulling the sled across the starting line. Finally, the racing dogs are lined up in a row, in pairs. They, too, know what's going on.

"Three—Two—One—Go!"

With gaping mouths, the huskies lunge down the trail, past the hundreds of clapping spectators lining the sides. For a moment it seems as if the sled, pulled ahead with such force, will leave gravity behind. Instinctively, Lutz Binzer steps on the brakes to synchronize the forward movement of the dogs as they tear down the trail. The steel teeth attached to the ends of the runners screech as they bite into the hard-packed snow, leaving behind a three-foot cloud of fine, white crystals. The maneuver works, and the huskies begin to move smoothly and evenly. With ears pressed back, they listen for their master's every command. "Haw!" he demands, with a firm but by no means loud voice. "Minni," the graceful lead dog, reacts immediately and turns, followed by the rest of the team. Lutz leans into the curve too, thereby exerting pressure against the stirrups on his runners. The vehicle, made of light, flexible wood and held together with elastic thongs, hugs the trail as it shoots around the curve. At the end of the curve, the dogs fall into a swift, efficient trot. Lutz Binzer takes a breath: he's made it over the first of the 1,000 kilometers.

About 30 daring men and women from Europe, North America, and Alaska sign up every year for this challenge called the Alpirod. In a good dozen stages, the race passes through Alpine winter sports areas in Italy, France, Austria, and Switzerland. It premiered in 1988.

Lutz Binzer is one of the most dedicated Alpirod enthusiasts. "The

Opposite page:
"Hike!" Lutz Binzer starting a race at Niederdorf, in the Southern Tyrol. (Alpirod, 1991)

Overleaf:
One of the most distinguishing features of the Siberian Husky is its beautiful almond-shaped eyes.

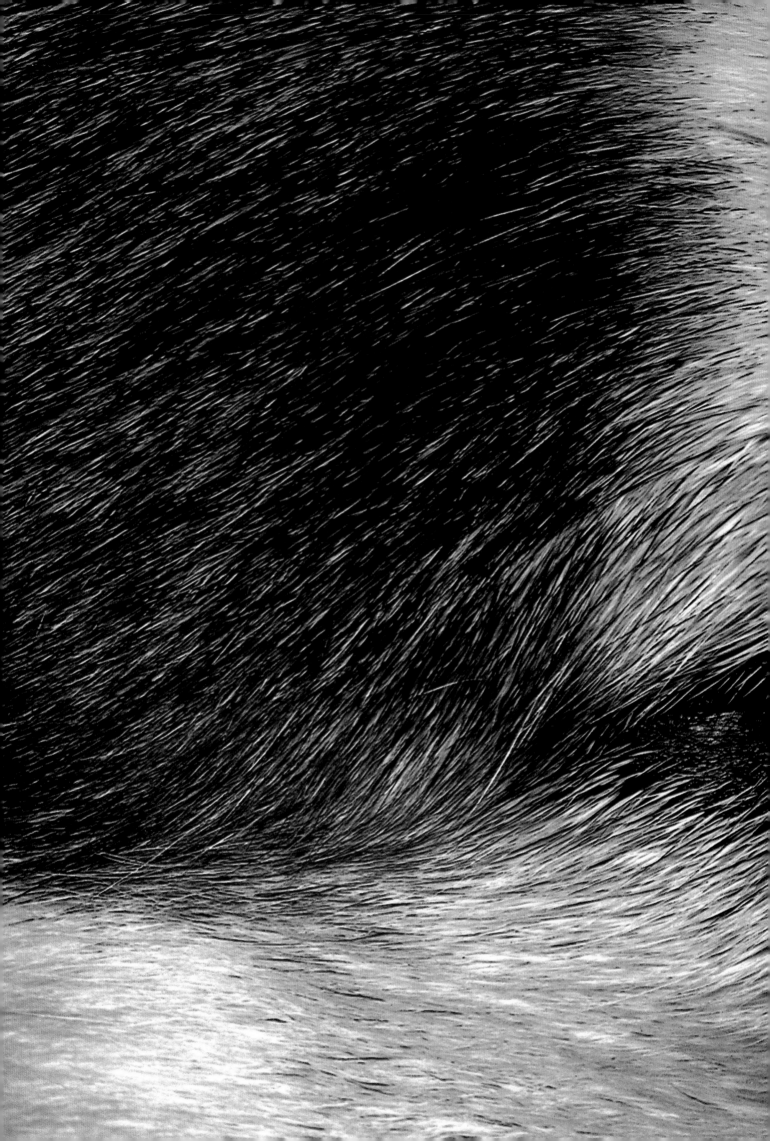

icy chase is one of the last challenges of our time," he likes to say. His friend Ulrike, on the other hand, faces a quite different challenge–she plays the thankless role of dog handler. She feeds and cares for the huskies and also takes care of Lutz, and she drives the dog boxes, beds, and equipment in a fully loaded small truck from one stage to the next. The truck serves as shelter and kitchen–it would simply be too complicated to pull into a different hotel every night.

In Lienz, I visit the two of them at the stake-out area. Ulrike is busy feeding the dogs, who are visibly tired from the lap they have just covered, with a special, energy-rich food. "She really has more to do than I do," admits Lutz, as he gives a sidelong teasing look at his friend. When the animals have finished their meal, Ulrike begins to grease and disinfect the huskies' paws. Then she puts on their little felt booties, which protect the dogs' heavily stressed feet during the race, but also reduce speed.

Five experienced veterinarians visit the 500 or so dogs participating in the Alpirod twice a day, removing sick or injured animals from the race. The person in charge is Chief Veterinarian Dominique Grandjean, a bearded combination of professor, master of the art of living, and entrepreneur. The first time I met the friendly Frenchman, he was holding a sort of pistol to the throat of a husky– and he pulled the trigger. With a hiss, the projectile penetrated the skin, but the dog did not even twitch. "Completely harmless," said Grandjean, trying to reassure me. "The dogs have to be coded." To do this, a microchip enclosed in Bioglass™ is inserted beneath the skin, where it remains for the life of the dog. It contains a code number that can be checked with a scanner at every stop-over. This tamper-proof control allows jurors to prevent illegal dog exchanges during the race. Grandjean is proud of his electronic device. "Soon we will be able to store complete health records and other important data on these chips," he prophesied, and my skeptical look encouraged him to share other visions: "We should implant these chips in people, too. With all your medical data stored beneath your skin, you'd really have something!" I was a little shocked, because there was no doubt that he was quite serious. In Paris, Grandjean is a university professor and works on the development of high-performance food for animals. In addition, he

Opposite page: *Monica d'Eliso and her team, photographed in a beautiful mountainous setting. (Alpirod, 1991)*

does the sled-dog races and, in the summer, he is involved in activities for windhounds (Afghan Hounds). Professor Grandjean is completely booked up. His wife, a stewardess with Air France, necessarily takes second place. "I see her maybe 40 days a year," he said, shrugging his shoulders. "But that's okay."

Every day there are drug checks. Blood is taken from the dogs–not the mushers–to check it in a special laboratory. The main purpose of the checks is to intimidate anyone who might be considering breaking the rules in order to win. This seems to work, for no participant has ever had to be disqualified because of drugs.

Change of scene: Niederdorf, Southern Tyrol. Lutz Binzer sees the steep hairpin turn ahead, but it is too late to brake. Minni cuts the obstacle too close, and the next pair of dogs goes off the trail. The heavily loaded sled snaps a couple of barricade posts like matchsticks and comes to a stop right in front of an almost six-foot-high rock embankment. Brakes screech on

Acrobatics. Frenchman Jean-Louis Parrour and his team at La Thuile in 1991. Mushers must be in top physical condition to withstand the rigors of a sled dog race.

the bare rock, sparks shoot out, and then the sled is airborne–for a fraction of a second there is an eerie stillness. Firmly clinging to the steering guide, Lutz sails over the slope and drops, still standing on the runners, and ends up with a thud in the new, white powder off to the side of the trail. "Whoow!" Lutz Binzer's cry of joy over his successful acrobatics is still ringing across the landscape as he carefully steadies the swaying rig and maneuvers it back onto the trail. Then the Allgäuer continues on the

way to Antholz as if nothing had happened. But he knows perfectly well that he has evaded disaster one more time.

Alaskan women play an outstanding role in the Alpirod. Libby Riddles, Deedee Jonrowe, Sherri Runyan–these names always turn up among the top ten. And Roxy Wright, too, has made her way up there to the top. In other big races, too, the women often defeat their male colleagues. The men take their revenge with cutting remarks on T-shirts, such as "Save the Males" or "Alaska–the land where men are still men and women win the Iditarod"–wryly making fun of themselves and harking back to the good old days. Clearly it is not physical strength that decides a sled dog race but rather the art of earning the unconditional trust of your animals, of providing them with optimal training, and of motivating them. When all is said and done, the competition is still won by the dogs.

A few days after the scare at Anholtz, Lutz Binzer's dream comes true. In Bessans he comes in sixth and is the best of the German participants. Later, I want to know how many more times he, a veteran of the Alpirod, would take part in this race. At first he looks puzzled– it is really a dumb question. Then, however, a smile passes over his face, and he says, "As long as there is snow."

Heini Winter and his 12 huskies experience sunrise in the mountains on the Italian-French border near La Thuile.
(Alpirod, 1991)

An Alpirod team takes a turn-off in Isolaccia. Landmarks along the trail ensure that a team finds its way back to the trail. (1991)

The Alpirod is one of the most strenuous sled dog races in the world. The perpetually uphill and downhill terrain makes extreme demands on the musher and the dogs. On uphill stretches, the musher–in this photo, it's Heini Winter at Livigno–has to help the dogs by pushing the sled, loaded down with equipment.

Signs like this one line the entire Alpirod trail. They indicate the way and warn of forks and dangerous spots.

At the end of an 80-kilometer-long, continuously uphill section of trail in the Engadin, the exhausted team arrives in Maloja. (Above: Alpirod, 1992; *below:* Alpirod, 1991)

The sun shines brightly on Finland's Lennart Lindqvist, pictured on the pass between Serre Chevalier, in France, and the Bardonecchia, in Italy. (Alpirod, 1991)

On the border. Because some sections of the Alpirod trail cross international boundaries, racers must theoretically deal with customs. Here, Canadian Grant Beck is crossing the border between Lienz, Austria, and Sexten, Italy. He carries his passport and his dogs' papers in the sled, just in case. If he were actually stopped

for a check, the time lost would be clocked by a referee who stands at the checkpoint, and later subtracted from the musher's total score. But with the temperature at 30° below zero, the curious border patrol is happy to let the team pass. (Alpirod, 1991)

Victorious. In 1992, the Alpirod was won for the first time by a European: Jacques Philip. In 1993, the Frenchman repeated his triumph. His recipe for success: He lives and trains in Alaska. (Above: *1991, Val d'Isere;* below: *1992, Lienz)*

Armen Khatchikian on the blue-ice trail out of Lienz. This Armenian-Italian racer and his brother direct a popular school for mushers. In 1992, the two inaugurated a new long-distance race–the "Transitalia," held in southern Italy.

An ice-covered husky at a stop point in Sexten. (Alpirod, 1991)

Lutz Binzer in the Upper Engadin, on the way from Maloja to Lavin. The freezing weather provides optimal racing conditions.

Donat Ertel at the end of the final stage. Although placing only in the last third, joy and relief shine on the racer's ice-covered face. Furthermore, because he has always finished the Alpirod, the German is automatically qualified for the Iditarod, the longest race in the world. (1991)

Morning shift. Frank Sihler, pictured here at the 1991 Alpirod in Lienz, was, until recently, involved in a husky farm in Bavaria, where adventure-seeking vacationers test their skills with dog sleds. Teams and equipment are provided, and after a week of training with professionals, "a musher is born."

Late shift. Dodo Perri on the trail to Sexten, in the Southern Tyrol. The night stages are among the high points of every Alpirod race; a small head lamp helps mushers find their way. Some leave them off, however, so as not to let competitors know where they are. (1991)

Before the race, every Alpirod husky gets a microchip implanted beneath its skin. The procedure, performed by Chief Veterinarian Dominique Grandjean, is nearly painless for the dog and has to be done only once: the chip stays in place for the dog's entire life.

With the help of a scanner, the code stored in the chip can be read at any time. This means that each dog can be correctly identified, preventing husky-changing during the race.

The electronic chip, only a few millimeters long, is encased in Bioglass™ to prevent rejection reactions and other complications.

At the 1992 Alpirod, "Open Sleeping" was introduced: musher and dogs have to spend a few nights out in the open, without outside help. With this innovation, the race orients itself more toward the Iditarod image.

The musher has to carry all essential equipment for Open Sleeping, as well as food for the dogs on his sled. Only straw and water are provided at the sleeping site. (Alpirod, 1992)

The winding stretches at Isolaccia are among the best and most demanding stages of the Alpirod. Where there are no guardrails, the musher had better have his team well in hand.

Light and shadows at Prags. (Alpirod, 1991)

Steady as a rock ... Hans Bos at Isolaccia. (Alpirod, 1991)

Monuments of Alpine civilization meet the Alpirod mushers at every step. At Isolaccia, even a dam serves as the trail.

*Tim White starting at Val d'Isere. At the 1991
Alpirod, this professional musher from
Minnesota barely won over his arch-opponent,
Grant Beck of Canada. The following year, he
was persuaded to enter the Transitalia, which
he won.*

*Turning technique. The Canadian Grant Beck
is one of the most internationally successful
mushers. In 1991, 1992, and 1993, he placed
second in the Alpirod. This photo shows him at
Zernez in 1992.*

On straight stretches, good teams like that of Toni Schmidt reach cruising speeds of almost 30 kilometers per hour. But the Alpirod is rarely as flat as it is here in the Upper Engadin. (1991)

Armen Khatchikian and his team on a scenic part of the trail in the Engadin. (Alpirod, 1991)

Pure sunshine. At the '91 Alpirod, the weather was like this not only at Livigno but also at all the other stages of the race as well.

110

*After the last stage at Maloja, Heini Winter
expresses gratitude to his lead dogs, which
brought him in tenth and–more importantly–
just ahead of his friend and favorite opponent,
Lutz Binzer. (Alpirod, 1991)*

*Even though the prize money doesn't cover the
costs of the trip, Heini Winter is pleased with
his trophy. Everyone who makes it to the end of
this race is a winner. (1991)*

Roxy Wright with lead dog "Alry" at Val d'Isère. Even in the strength-sapping Alpirod, female mushers are allowed no handicap at all over the male competition. Nevertheless, in 1990, this Alaska resident won first place, and the following year, third place.

Libby Riddles at the finishing line at Maloja. Although first place in the Alpirod has eluded her, the teacher from Alaska has long been in the annals of sled dog racing: in 1985, she was the first woman in the world to win the legendary Iditarod.

Sherri Runyan of Alaska pushes her sled uphill with all her might. (Alpirod, 1991)

Whoosh! At the 1991 Alpirod, the first stage, set at La Thuile, was the most difficult. Here, Andrea Caglieris of Italy shows her stuff.

Tunnel effect at Isolaccia. The dogs must literally have blind faith in the musher—here, Dodo Perri.
(1991)

Crash! Above La Thuile, Hans Bos loses his balance and his sled turns over. The Netherlander keeps an iron grip on the handlebars and is pulled along. Finally, he manages to get his team to stop in the deep snow off to the side of the trail. (Alpirod, 1991)

All of a sudden…Thierry Sirer of France also struggles over rocks and stones on the much-too-narrow trail at La Thuile. He not only knocks down a barrier but also takes a little tree with him–no feather in the cap of the trail planner. (Alpirod, 1991)

A rookie in action. Not all Alpirod mushers are as experienced as one might expect. You always find novices who run a good distance behind the others—and no wonder, when you see the tug lines as slack as

they are in this picture. Some of these rookies are disqualified after just a few stages because they've exceeded the alloted times. (1991)

Sickbay. One of Hans Gatt's dogs wore himself out on the 79-kilometer stretch from Lavin to Maloja and had to finish out that stage in the sled sack. (Alpirod, 1992)

Drug testing. After every stage, a team chosen at random gets checked. A veterinarian takes blood from the dogs and tests it in a special laboratory in Milan. Plus side: For a long time now, not a single case of drugging has come to light. (Alpirod, 1991)

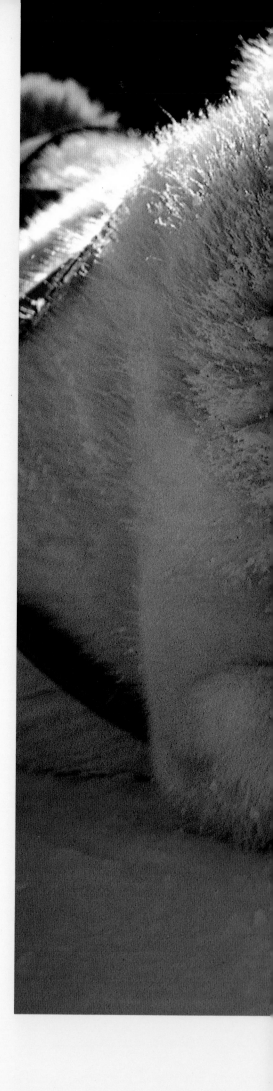

A hungry Alaskan Husky devours a piece of frozen salmon. (Alpirod, 1991)

The old man and the trail. Norman D. Vaughan is one of the most remarkable personalities that the sled dog sport has ever produced. Born in December 1905, the musher and adventurer was a member of numerous polar expeditions–among others, with Richard E. Byrd on his first Antarctic exploration in 1929. Vaughan was responsible for the more than 90 sled dogs on that exploration. In 1990, at the age of 84, Vaughan took part in the

Iditarod and finished the longest sled dog race in the world normally: after 21 days. Ten months later, he ran the Alpirod, but had to stop after the first stage. Still, when someone asks the old-timer the frequent question, "When are you going to hang it up?" he gives the familiar answer, "When I'm old enough."

Happy trails...because every meter is worth the effort. (Jean-Louis Parrour in the Engadin, Alpirod, 1991).

Classes and Breeds

Sled dog sports are enjoying a growing popularity in Europe. There are about 1,000 active members in the German sled dog organization alone. Especially popular are the sprint races, which are held in various categories. Preferably, you begin with small teams in the four-dog and six-dog classes (track length about 7 to 12 kilometers). People who can afford larger kennels try the eight-dog class and run tracks of about 15 kilometers in length. The king of events is the open class, with more than eight dogs pulling the sled and trails about 25 kilometers long. In addition, Europe also has medium-distance races, such as the Silvretta 3000, and a few long-distance races.

Until recently, most of the team dogs were purebreds such as Siberian Huskies, Alaskan Malamutes, or Samoyeds. Now, more and more mushers are switching to Alaskan Huskies. This name describes the fastest (and they're not even purebred!) sled dogs in the world. Originating in Alaska, they were Indian dogs, which have since been bred for racing. Today, they are popular in Europe too. The features to look for are primarily performance, character, and resilience; external features, of no importance for racing, are second in rank and may vary. Thus, these dogs differ widely in appearance: large and small, floppy or perky ears, light

Alaskan Huskies at Val d'Isère. (Alpirod, 1991)

and dark, short–and long-haired– anything is possible as long as the animal is good for sled work. By now, Alaskan Huskies have carried the day with almost all internationally successful mushers, setting new standards for the sport in the process. You find them everywhere, at open sprint races and at the Iditarod as well. In personality, these dogs are less complicated than the Siberian Husky, but still, you should think it over very carefully before choosing such an action-loving dog for a family pet.

Opposite page: *A winner. Anja Hörmann with her lead dog on the way up at Haidmühle. (Third place, eight-dog class, 1993)*

The Samoyed's ancestors guarded and herded reindeer.

The Alaskan Malamute is the largest of the sled dogs and is employed for heavier loads over shorter distances.

SAMOYED

Samoyeds were the first Nordic dogs to make a public name for themselves. They were mentioned in travel reports way back at the beginning of the 18th century–the name probably referred to any dog between Iran and Northern Russia that accompanied the nomadic people called the Samoyeds on their hunts and guarded their reindeer. When moving from place to place, people quite naturally harnessed the dogs to sleds.

In 1889, the Englishman Robert Scott brought the first of these dogs to Europe, where they soon were much appreciated. Over years of breeding, the variety, heterogeneous at first, was evened out; finally, all that remained were animals with dense, white coats. Nowadays, Samoyeds are in the sled dog category and also appear in races. Males have a shoulder height of about 24 inches; eyes are dark brown.

Samoyeds do not stand out as team dogs. Although extremely friendly with humans, they are headstrong and need an experienced owner.

ALASKAN MALAMUTE

Once you have seen this powerful dog at work, you will quickly understand why the Alaskan Malamute entered sled dog history as the "freight train of the North." Named after a group of Indians living in northwest Alaska, the Malamute also gained glory as a racer during the gold rush and pioneer days. It was also crossed so intensively with other types of dogs that the original race practically disappeared. Luckily, a few typical specimens were bred further, preserving the strain.

Shoulder height for males is about 25 inches; weight should be about 85 pounds. The eyes are brown and should be as dark as possible. With measurements like these, Malamutes are not as fast as the agile Siberian Huskies, but they can pull heavier loads.

Malamutes do not make good watchdogs–they are friendly toward anyone! As team dogs, however, they have kept a certain independence, and they require strict training.

The Siberian Husky excels as a sled dog par excellence: no other purebred dog compares for endurance and consistency.

The Greenland Dog developed from intense natural selection and appears the most wolf-like of all purebred sled dogs.

SIBERIAN HUSKY

The Siberian Husky is the fastest and most popular purebred sled dog. Originally from northeastern Siberia, it is a favorite nowadays primarily in North America and Central Europe, as a work and show dog.

At the beginning of this century, the Siberian Husky made its way to Alaska, where, because of its more delicate appearance (shoulder height to about 24 inches, weight to about 60 pounds) in comparison with the Alaskan Malamute, people made fun of it. This changed, however, when the newcomers turned out to be unbelievably fast.

Siberian Huskies have the face mask typical of sled dogs, and their coats are dense and medium long. Their almond-shaped eyes, set slightly at an angle, are either ice blue or brown; sometimes a dog can have one of each. These dogs are extremely friendly team animals without the qualities of a watchdog. If you keep one as a family pet, treat it like any sled dog and give it plenty of exercise and good training.

GREENLAND DOG

This old breed of sled dog is a descendant of the Greenland Eskimo Dog, which helped its owners hunt and also pulled loads. Beautifully adapted to the harsh existence in its native lands and subject to relentless selection, in appearance and behavior it is quite similar to its ancestral father, the wolf, while being at the same time thoroughly attached to humans.

Greenlands introduced into Europe were first "civilized" through many generations of regulated breeding. Nevertheless, even these lines have retained a large measure of their headstrong behavior.

Greenlands have a shoulder height of about 24 inches and all types of coat markings–only albinos are not permitted. The dark eyes of this sturdy animal are set at an angle.

Greenlands do not make good house pets and need particularly strict handlers, people who, in every situation, can maintain their stance as "alpha animal."

Clubs and Organizations

In sled dog sports, as in most other sports, responsible "umbrella" organizations try hard to oversee the activities of countless clubs (some in competition with one another). The following summary should provide some clarity in this regard.

We should differentiate between open and closed sled dog clubs. The open ones admit all types of dogs, including animals that are not purebreds. Consequently, their members primarily use Alaskan Huskies. In contrast, the members of the closed clubs mostly own purebred sled dog teams; the only huskies admitted to the starting line are those with a recognized pedigree. Open and closed clubs each tend to think that they have the "true science," but don't let that bother you.

OPEN SLED DOG SPORTING CLUBS

(for all sled dogs, even mixed breeds)

DSSV: Deutscher Schlittenhunde-Sport-Verband (German Sled Dog Sport Club).

ESDRA: European Sled Dog Racing Association– Organization for European sled dog sports; sponsors, for example, the open European Sprint Championship.

IFSS: International Federation of Sled Dog Sports– World organization for sled dog sports; sponsors of the World Championship Sprint.

ISDRA: International Sled Dog Racing Association– North American organization for sled dog sports.

MSVÖ: Musher-Sport-Verband-Österreich–The Austrian sled dog sport organization.

SVS: Schweizerischer Verband für Schlittenhundesport (Swiss Society for Sled Dog Sports).

TCE: Trail Club of Europe–An organization founded in Switzerland; sponsors races in many European countries.

CLOSED SLED DOG SPORTS CLUBS

(only for purebred sled dogs with pedigrees)

AGSD: Arbeits-Gemeinschaft Schlittenhundesport Deutschland (Association of German Sled Dog Sports).

FISTC: Fédération Internationale de Sport de Traîneau Chiens–European organization that sponsors the European World Championship for purebred dogs.

ÖSHS: Österreichischer Schlitten-Hunde-Sportclub (Austrian Sled Dog Sport Club).

SKS: Schweizerischer Klub für Schlittenhundesport (Austrian Club for Sled Dog Sports).

SSK: Schweizerischer Schlittenhundesport-Klub (Sled Dog Sport Club of Switzerland).

CLUBS FOR BREEDERS OF PUREBRED DOGS

AKC: American Kennel Club– American organization for purebred dogs.

DCNH: Deutscher Club für Nordische Hunde (Nordic Dog Club of Germany).

FCI: Fédération Cynologique Internationale– European organization for national cynology clubs.

ÖCNH: Österreichischer Club für Nordische Hunde (Nordic Dog Club of Austria).

ÖKV: Österreichischer Kynologen-Verband–Austrian organization for cynology.

SKG: Schweizerischer Kynologische Gesellschaft– Swiss organization for cynology.

SKNH: Schweizerischer Klub für Nordische Hunde– Nordic Dog Club of Switzerland.

VDH: Verband für das Deutsche Hundewesen–German organization for cynology.

IMPORTANT ADDRESSES

AGSD: Arbeitsgemeinschaft Schlittenhundesport Deutschland e.V., Obere Mahlgasse 4, D-55270 Ober-Olm, Tel. (0 61 36) 8 96 91, Fax (0 61 36) 8 90 98

DSSV: Deutscher Schlittenhundesport Verband e.V., Geschaftsstelle, St.-Ulrich-Strasse 19a, D-86343 Konigsbrunn, Tel. (0 82 31) 52 60, Fax (0 82 31) 8 84 10

Races and Championships

Sled dog races are held in almost every country in Europe. In Germany alone there are more than 50 each year. It is hardly possible to compile a complete, accurate list for seasons to come because dates and locations vary from year to year, and new races are always being added to the list. Sprint races, all in all, are usually no longer than 60 kilometers. Medium-distance races range from 150 to 500 kilometers, and everything over that falls into the long-distance category.

The magazines *Husky*, *Trail*, and *Schlittenhund* publish in their fall and winter issues the dates for almost all of the European sprint, medium-distance, and long-distance races. In addition, the racing calendars of the various national dog-sled clubs also provide information; mailing addresses for these organizations can be found in the magazines themselves. It is not particularly difficult, then, to locate a race in your own vicinity. Here are just a few selected events:

SPRINT RACES

Sprint races are always held on the weekend: the first running on Saturday, the second on Sunday; the times are added up.

Bad Mitterndorf: This open Austrian race is a special favorite of the public. Since Bad Mitterndorf is also often the site of a championship and of one of the components of series such as the Pedigree Pal Trophy, you usually find the international elite of mushers there (sponsors: MSVO, dates in *Husky*).

Other places where open sled dog races are commonly found:
   ...in Germany: Buchenberg, Haidmühle, Oberwiesenthal, Wallgau
   ...in Austria: Kötschach-Mauthen, Nassereith, Rauris
   ...in Switzerland: Sils

Important sites for purebred sled dog races:
   ...in Germany: Brotterode (Long-trail qualification)
   ...in Austria: Goldegg, Kossen
   ...in Switzerland: Andermatt

Pedigree Pal Trophy: This is a season-long series of open individual races held in four countries (Germany, Austria, Switzerland, and Italy). Thanks to large sponsor contributions, these races are extremely attractive for both participants and spectators (information can be obtained from DSSV and *Husky*).

European Championships: European championships take place once a year. Open and closed clubs have separate championships, so do not confuse them. (Agencies are ESDRA and FISTC; information on dates can be found in the professional journals or obtained from DSSV or AGSD.)

World Championship: The Open World Championship covers three days of racing (Friday-Sunday) and is held alternately in Europe and North America (Alaska) —for example— in 1993 in Alaska and in 1994 in Germany for the first time. (Sponsor: IFSS; information on dates available in sled dog periodicals or from the DSSV.)

LONG-DISTANCE RACES

Alpirod: This Alpine marathon takes place in about a dozen stages and traverses some of the most beautiful winter-sport country in Italy, France, Austria, and Switzerland. The total length is up to 1,000 kilometers, and among the participants are some of the best long-distance mushers of Europe and North America. (Information: Authentika SA ; 14, Rue LaFayette; F-75000 Paris; Tel. 0033-1-48 01 98 50; Fax 0033-1-42 69 68 22.)

Other long-distance races are the Transitalia (open) and the Transalpin (purebred).

Photo Tips for Sled Dog Races

If you attend a sled dog race, be sure to take home a few good photographs. This is really not so hard to do. For the hobby photographer, the saying "less is more" is particularly true. The lighter the equipment, the easier it is to be at the right place at the right time. Ordinary zoom lenses with focal lengths of 28-80 and 80-200 millimeters cover most of the situations that arise at sled dog races. On occasion, this basic equipment can be expanded downward with a super-wide-angle lens (i.e., 20 mm) and upward with a telephoto lens with a focal distance of 300 mm or more.

Usually there is more than enough snow covering the racing sites, so you can rely on slower and therefore smaller and less expensive lenses. For the same reason, it is best to use low-sensitivity film (ISO 50 or ISO 100), whose high level of sharpness and color saturation promise the best results. For prints, Kodak's Ektar 100 and Fuji's Reala have proved best. If you would rather work with slide film, the following are outstanding (but unfortunately, not inexpensive): Fuji Velvia (ISO 50) and Fuji RD 100 (with the same color specification). Results just as good can be obtained with Kodak's Ektachrome Elite Film (sensitivity 50-400). Less acceptable are the Kodachrome films–Kodachrome 200, in particular, tends to be greenish and yellowish in snow. Ultimately, however, this may all be a matter of taste. "Go for the subject!" is a rule you hear over and over in film schools. For sled dog races, this is especially true. Particularly if you are using a wide-angle lens, go after the huskies before and after the race–the ambience of a race is always good for a few interesting shots. In addition, include some landscape in a shot of a running team.

On the trail, closeups are usually permitted only to accredited sports photographers, and often they irresponsibly annoy passing teams. To show respect for all participants, the use of telephoto lenses is advisable. With them, you can catch the energy and strength of a team in action beautifully, providing you have chosen a shutter speed of 1/500 or less. It is best to position yourself behind a curve close to the ground. A photo taken from this angle gives the impression that the huskies are bearing down right on the photographer.

Impressive shots also may include other subjects taken from the side; you can use a normal lens (for example, 50 mm) for this. With a shutter speed of 1/30 or 1/15, follow the passing subject with the viewfinder–background and moving parts such as the dogs' feet disappear, but the rest stays fairly sharp if you do it right. Don't give up here: even professionals sometimes have to try a swing shot ten times or more to get one good picture.

In the strongly contrasting winter landscape, the photographer will necessarily have to wrestle with problems of lighting, especially when working with slide film.

A high-speed 300-mm telephoto lens with internal focusing makes it easy to take split-second action photos. Good pictures at sled dog races are also possible with equipment that is considerably less expensive.

People using ordinary reflex cameras should not rely on their mid-tone integral measurement, which in white snow always tends markedly toward under-lighting

(only a few cameras with multi-field measurement and built-in fuzzy logic can correct the lighting on their own in such situations). Therefore, we give the following rule of thumb: point your camera toward the white snow and measure the light through the viewfinder (integrated or spot measurement). If you raise the exposure two aperture openings above the value obtained, you will usually get good results. For example: you take a reading from the snow and get an aperture opening of 11 at 1/500. The correct setting would then be an aperture of 5.6 at 1/500 second. If you want to be certain, you can, of course, use a light meter.

Most of the photographs used in this book were taken with Contax cameras on 35-millimeter film; some shots were produced using 4.5 x 6 cm and 6 x 6 cm. Lenses between 18 and 500 millimeters were used, as well as various electronic flashes with guide numbers between 30 and 60. In this case, it has turned out to be especially practical to use monopods and–for working close to the ground–an angle viewfinder.

Husky ABCs

The modern sport of sled dog racing developed in North America and Alaska, and this fact has implications for the special terms used, even in Europe. What follows is a list of the most important sled-dog racing terms.

GENERAL RACING TERMS

dog driver–In Canada and Alaska, commonly used term for musher.

dog handler–Helper who works with the musher at races to take care of the dogs.

dog team–International term.

double lead–See lead dog.

Good mushing!–International expression, applied to dog teams.

lead dog–Runs at the head of the team. Sometimes there are two lead dogs, harnessed side by side (double lead).

musher–Common term for the driver of a sled dog team, probably derived from the French word "marcher," which means to walk or to go.

musher meeting–Meeting of mushers with race officials just before the competition begins; all important information about the race is given out here.

point dogs–In the USA (but not in Alaska), common synonym for swing dogs.

show dog–Purebred sled dog raised for shows.

swing dog–The two dogs harnessed directly behind the lead dog; usually extremely fast animals.

team dogs–All the dogs harnessed between the swing dogs and the wheel dogs.

trail–Path traveled by a dog team in a race or during training.

wheel dogs–The two dogs harnessed directly to the front of the sled.

yearling–Husky that has completed its first year of life.

COMMANDS

Gee!–Right.

Haw!–Left.

Come gee!–180-degree turn to the right.

Come haw!–180-degree turn to the left.

Hike!–Permission to run loose.

Whoa!–Command to stop, but usually has little effect.

HARNESS VARIATIONS

double hitch–See gang hitch.

fan hitch–Fan-shaped team: each individual dog is attached to the sled by a separate line.

gang hitch–Racing harness, the dogs run in pairs side by side. The lead dog is attached directly to the central main gang line; the other animals are connected to the gang line by short tug lines.

tandem hitch–See gang hitch.

single-tandem hitch–Pulka harness; all the dogs run singly one behind the other, with tug poles or lines to the left and right of them.

EQUIPMENT AND SUPPLIES

basket–Loading surface of the sled, on which the sled sack is found. Any injured dog is carried to the finish line in the sled sack, and in long-distance races, the basket also holds the necessary equipment.

booties–Little fabric covers (with Velcro closures) for the dogs' feet, to protect them from injury. In long distance races, a team often needs more than a hundred of these.

bridle–Device at the front end of the sled to which the gang line is attached with a hitch.

bumper–See brush bow.

brush bow–Curved wooden bumper-like structure at the front end of the sled, which protects the dogs from injury and the sled from damage.

dog pack–Saddle bags for ski dogs, very practical for trips.

gang line–Central tug line, fastened to the sled. The sled dogs are attached to the gang line by means of tug lines and neck lines. Also called tow line.

handle bar–The musher grips these to hold on to the sled.

harness–Apparatus for attaching the dogs to the sled.

hook–Sled brake, foot activated.

neck line–Line connecting the neck band with the gang line or the neck bands of two lead dogs with each other.

panic snap–Security hook; in an emergency, releases in a fraction of a second.

pulka–The frame, made of wood or a man-made material, used in the Scandinavian sport of the same name; pulled along the trail by sled dogs. The dogs are connected to the pulka by means of tug poles (single tandem hitch); the musher, on touring skis, follows behind and is also connected to the sled by means of a line. The number of dogs varies, but the weight of the pulka is fixed: 20 kilograms per team, 15 for one dog. Similar to pulka driving is skijoring, in which the musher, also on skis, is pulled directly by the dog.

runner–Sled runner; must be waxed like skis.

schneeanker–Steel hook fastened to the sled with a rope, for anchoring the sled in the snow; may also be hooked to a stable tree or post.

stake-out–Device made of chains and wire cable, used in racing, training, or touring, for tying up a whole team of huskies out in the open before the start. From a long main chain, shorter chains or cables for each dog branch off at regular intervals: this keeps rival animals from getting into fights.

toboggan–Flat sled used by northern Canadian Indians; today, its modern form serves as a transport and racing sled in long-distance races.

tug line–Secondary tug line, attaches each dog to the gang line.

Suggested Reading

All-Breed Dog Books From T.F.H.

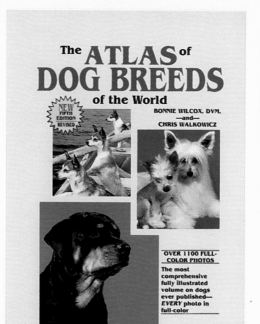

TS-175, 896 pp
Over 1300 color
photos

H-1106, 544 pp
Over 400 color photos

H-1091, 912 pp
Over 1100 color photos

Sled Dog Books from T.F.H.

TS-148, 512 pp
Over 500 color photos

H-954, 384 pp
Over 300 photos

KW-072, 192 pp
Over 175 color photos

PS-855, 288 pp
Over 100 color photos

  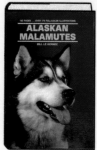

KW-160, 192 pp
Over 175 color photos

PS-737, 415 pp
Over 300 photos

KW-094, 192 pp
Over 175 color photos

T.F.H. Publications, Inc., the world's largest publisher of pet animal books, offers the most comprehensive and colorful selection of dog books. T.F.H. books are available at pet shops everywhere.

Index

Page numbers in boldface refer to illustrations.